Zen Unleashed

Zen unleashed

Everyday Buddhist Wisdom from Man's Best Friend

By Tim Macejak and
Sheila the Zen Dog

Illustrations by Bud Podrazik

BEAVER'S POND
PRESS

ISBN: 978-1-59298-990-4
Library of Congress Control Number: 2013904185

Printed in the United States of America
Designed by Mayfly Design and Typeset in Arno Pro
Cover watercolor work by Sue Strandberg
First Printing: 2013

17   16   15   14   13   5   4   3   2   1

Beaver's Pond Press, Inc.
7108 Ohms Lane
Edina, Minnesota 55439
(952) 829-8818
www.BeaversPondPress.com

To order, visit www.BeaversPondBooks.com
or call (800) 901-3480. Reseller discounts available.

To my Master's wife Teresa

for supporting him in everything he does,
and throwing me popcorn from time to time.

Introduction

Hi! My name is Sheila. I'm an eight-year-old mutt, and I have a secret.

It's a secret that makes my tail wag and allows me to run free with abandon and joy. It also allows me to live with myself after I'm bad and dump the garbage over. It's a secret that all dogs share, and now I'm spilling the beans to you.

Dogs are Zen Buddhists.

It's true! And as long as I'm telling it like it is, here's another secret: cats can practice Zen. So can squirrels. People can, too. Whether you're religious or not, Zen doesn't ask you to change what you believe. It's simply a way of living that involves being awake in the moment and letting go of your attachments. I do it every day, and so can you.

In this book, I use pictures, haiku poetry, and my own experiences to cover some of the basics of Buddhism, a 2,500-year-old teaching founded by a dog lover called the Buddha. Well, I'm just assuming he was a dog lover. His teachings emphasize the dog-like view that we are happiest when we go with the flow in a constantly changing world.

After revealing what I know about Buddhism, I'll dig into some key points of Zen practice, a school of Buddhism that is the foundation of a dog's life. Zen teaching emphasizes a daily practice of living in the now, being open to life as it is.

So join me as I share the experiences of life with my Master. (Yes, call me old fashioned, but I do prefer the title *Master* over the politically correct but biologically impossible *Dad*.) Feel free to read this book from front to back, in order. That's what cats would do. Or just pick it up and read from any old spot. That's what dogs would do. Whether you're a cat or a dog at heart, I hope my life experiences can help you wag your own tail vigorously and often!

PART ONE

. . . .

The Bare Bones of Buddhism

ZEN UNLEASHED

. . . .

Papers by the door
They're so icky; I wake up
And bark to go out

. . . .

Who Was the Buddha?

As this haiku poem illustrates, every dog has a great awakening in his or her life. There comes a day when you're a puppy about to relieve yourself on some newspapers, and you suddenly think, "Whoa, this is just craaaaaazy — I need to do my business outside." This changes your whole life.

Yet awakenings aren't limited to dogs. Around the year 530 BCE, a man by the name of Siddhartha Gautama experienced the greatest of awakenings. For the next forty-five years, he taught others about his experience. During this time, when asked if he was a god, he would reply, "No, I am awake." Consequently, he began to be called "the Buddha," which means "the Awakened One."

So the Buddha wasn't a god, but rather a person just like you or me—well, okay, not me, since I'm a dog.

ZEN UNLEASHED

. . . .

The rays of the sun
Glorious beams from heaven
Give warmth to my life

. . . .

Does God Exist?

Even though the Buddha wasn't a god, people would still ask him about the existence of gods in general. He always refused to answer these questions. He didn't say gods exist, and he didn't say gods don't exist. Instead, he replied that he was only interested in talking about suffering in this life, its causes, and how we can escape it.

By refusing to discuss the topic of God, the Buddha left belief or nonbelief up to us. Personally, I think that basking in a nice patch of sunshine—drowsy, lazy, fuzzy, comforting sunshine—has a spiritual quality that cannot be completely explained by science.

ZEN UNLEASHED

. . . .

Sleep in all year long
Then come winter, get hitched to
White, frozen dogsled

. . . .

The Middle Way

The Buddha's path to his awakening was colored by opposite experiences. He was born into a wealthy family and was pampered in his youth. As he grew older, he became troubled by the existence of sickness, old age, and death. He eventually left home on a spiritual quest and joined a group of monks who were following an extreme practice of self-denial—the complete opposite of the life he had just been leading. However, after he almost died from starvation, the Buddha realized he needed to follow a path that avoided both extremes. Because this path travels between indulgence and denial, sometimes Buddhism is dubbed "the middle way."

So on the one hand, lazing around the house all day doing nothing—that's no good. On the other hand, being in an endless dogsled race in Alaska with temperatures well below zero, winds that cause complete loss of visibility, pulling a packed sled through mountain ranges, dense forests, and frozen rivers, with somebody yelling, "Mush!" at you all day long—whoa!—that's no good, either.

ZEN UNLEASHED

. . . .

Bark at everyone
Or lie down for tummy rubs
How shall I greet life?

. . . .

The Middle Way and Barking

If we bark at everyone, we might get a one-way trip to the pound. If we're always lying down for tummy rubs, we might get stepped on by burglars. Which is better? Looks like maybe we need to find a middle path.

Although the Buddha's teaching about the middle way originally pertained to the extremes of overindulgence and austerity, this teaching applies to everything in life. Pay attention to extremes developing in your own life. If too much running and playing is wearing you down, get some sleep. If you're sleeping too much, run and play more. As for barking, I try to keep it to what Master calls "tolerable levels."

ZEN UNLEASHED

. . . .

Sunshine, warm breeze, gnats
I lie under the oak tree
Watching Master mow

. . . .

The Buddha's Inspiration

When the Buddha realized that the path of extreme self-denial was not the way to go, he pondered what to do next. He then remembered a time in his life when he had felt truly at peace. It was when he was a small boy sitting under a tree on a sunny day, doing nothing but watching his father plow.

Up until this point, he had tried many different types of meditation that were common in India at the time. From here on, however, the Buddha began to base his meditation on this experience of *just being*. This meditation ultimately led to the Buddha's great awakening and forty-five years of teaching.

Once, when watching Master mow the lawn as I sat under a tree, I had an experience of great peace, just like the young Buddha. Actually, I fell asleep while Master was mowing, which was very, very wonderful.

ZEN UNLEASHED

. . . .

Oh boy it's dog food
I stand firm, growl, and protect
This sloppy, wet mess

. . . .

The First Noble Truth

Shortly after the Buddha's awakening, he delivered his first sermon. In this sermon he outlined what are called the four noble truths.

The Buddha's first noble truth was that life is *dukha*, which is often translated as "suffering." A better translation might be "unsatisfactory," as the word includes the whole range of misfortunes, from being hit by a car, to being lost and not able to find your way back home, to just having fleas.

Dissatisfaction also includes the positive things in life. Since nothing is permanent, we suffer even when things go well. This is because we fear losing what we have. During the course of a fine meal, I get quite protective when anyone comes near. Sometimes I even growl. Indeed, suffering touches everyone and everything, even dogs at the dinner bowl.

ZEN UNLEASHED

. . . .

I follow Master
From room to room, smelling food
Begging for a treat

. . . .

The Second Noble Truth

The Buddha's second noble truth is that suffering is caused by desire. This feels counterintuitive. It seems that when we satisfy our desires, we are happy.

Right?

Not exactly. Unfortunately, desire never ends. I remember when I used to beg for "people food." After I got my treat, it wasn't long before I wanted more. My happiness was temporary and quickly transformed into more desire. Eventually, Master got tired of me begging all the time, so he cut me off cold.

As you can imagine, I then experienced even more suffering.

ZEN UNLEASHED

. . . .

The greasy, balding
Ragged, flea-bitten tomcat
Scurries here, then there

. . . .

The Third and Fourth Noble Truths

In the Buddha's third noble truth, he declares that the situation is not hopeless. There is a release from the suffering, or dissatisfaction, that he has talked about.

In the fourth noble truth, he outlines the way toward that release, which he calls the eightfold path. The eightfold path can be understood as an interconnected network of qualities to be developed. Two aspects of the path involve the development of wisdom (right view and right intention). Three aspects deal with ethical conduct (right speech, right action, and right livelihood). The final three aspects of the path focus on mental development and meditation (right effort, right mindfulness, and right concentration). If this seems complex to you, you aren't alone. The Buddha discussed the eightfold path for forty-five years.

The third noble truth inspires us to try to do better, and the fourth noble truth gives us a guide as to how. With these truths in mind, I will try to rewrite my judgmental haiku about the tomcat.

. . . .

Slightly soiled, mildly
Unkempt, the nice kitty takes
Forever to choose

. . . .

Okay, it's a work in progress.

ZEN UNLEASHED

························

On my morning walk
A new, bright pink fire hydrant
I feel unsettled

························

The Teaching of Impermanence and No-Self

The Buddha taught that nothing is permanent. This imper-manence touches everything, including the minutiae of life—like the color of fire hydrants. Speaking as a dog, the new rainbow colors certainly take some getting used to!

From the Buddha's teaching of impermanence came his teaching that the self does not exist. This teaching may seem odd, since we certainly feel as if we exist. However, what the Buddha specifically taught was that there is no permanent, unchanging self that exists independently and separate from the rest of the universe.

So, on the one hand, you definitely do exist. On the other hand, you are already different from who you were just five minutes ago, as is the universe.

ZEN UNLEASHED

Lightning and thunder
I shiver in fear; Master
Smiles, explains physics

. . . .

The First Two Jewels: Buddha and Dharma

As a Buddhist, one vows to "take refuge" in the Three Jewels. The first two Jewels are Buddha and Dharma. Taking refuge in the Buddha means to be inspired by the historical Buddha as a teacher, as well as all teachers we may meet. To take refuge in the Dharma means to be inspired by the Buddha's teachings, as well as any teachings we may encounter in our life.

A real life example? Thunderstorms. During them, I feel a tad stressed. But then there is Master, who, like the Buddha, inspires me with his calmness. Then he provides teaching: cold fronts, electricity, sound waves. What a great comfort to have things explained!

If Master instead were to crawl under the bed and start howling, or if he tried to dig a hole in the carpet with his bare hands, I can't imagine what I'd do. Probably panic.

ZEN UNLEASHED

. . . .

"Fetch shoes," Master cries
In my mouth I grab my leash
An honest mistake

. . . .

The Third Jewel: Sangha

The third of the Three Jewels is *Sangha*, the community of fellow Buddhist practitioners. To take refuge in the Sangha is to support others and to be supported by others.

Through either circumstances or choice, many Buddhists maintain a solitary meditative practice at home. This is fine, but Buddhists should also make an effort to have at least occasional contact with not only a Buddhist teacher, but also other Buddhists. There is a type of friendly, nonthreatening spiritual feedback that only sangha members can give each other.

Like when Master told me to fetch his shoes. Whoa! That wasn't going to happen. As his sangha buddy, I needed to redirect his behavior to something more thoughtful. So I stood there with a leash in my mouth, tail wagging. Master chuckled, then got his shoes for himself before taking me on a wonderful walk through town. Then, as my sangha buddy, he encouraged me to stay on the sidewalk and off people's lawns.

ZEN UNLEASHED

Exactly the same
Groomed, unkempt, male, or female
To the dogs at play

. . . .

The Buddha's Acceptance of Women and All Social Classes

Have you ever been to a dog park? Dogs aren't too picky about whom they play with. Sometimes their owners have concerns, though. "Why doesn't that dog have a collar? Is it a stray? Look, that dog has fleas!"

When people are worried or afraid, they try to keep dogs separated. Dogs don't pay much attention to the distinctions that bother people; we'll play with pretty much anybody.

The Buddha played with pretty much anybody, too. After his enlightenment, he took strong stands against the cultural norms of his time. First, he rejected the caste system, a belief that people were born into certain stations in life and were destined to remain there. Instead, he welcomed all castes into the Sangha, including the lowest members, called the Untouchables. As if that hadn't caused enough controversy, he then took on the task of admitting women into the Sangha, promoting the idea that they were equally capable of enlightenment as men were.

ZEN UNLEASHED

. . . .

Stopping in its tracks
Back arching, fur like stiff spikes
This cat becomes huge

. . . .

Verify All Teachings

An ancient legend says that cats double in size when threatened. It makes sense that they could, doesn't it? Some of my best doggie friends have told me they can grow like this. I've also seen it written in a holy book, and a prominent spiritual teacher has claimed it to be true.

Are you now a believer, too? Well, the Buddha taught people not to believe what they couldn't verify for themselves. He said, "Don't go by reports, or legend, or traditions, or scripture, by logical conjecture, by inference, by analogies, by consistency with your own views, by probability, or because it is said by your teacher." The Buddha said this especially applied to his own teachings. He encouraged us all to directly experience and verify what he taught, rather than to take his teachings on faith.

ZEN UNLEASHED

. . . .

A golden turkey!
Who left it? How big is it?
How much should I take?

. . . .

Questions About the Nature of the Universe

This haiku is inspired by a true story. One day I wandered into the kitchen to discover a wonderful, fragrant Thanksgiving turkey sitting unattended on the table. Instead of pulling it to the floor, I started contemplating a bunch of useless questions, wondering how it got there and trying to decide if it was bigger than last year's turkey. Before long, Master came in and carried the wonderful meal off.

The Buddha understood the futility of useless questions. Once, a student expressed frustration that the Buddha always refused to answer his questions about the nature of the universe—how big was it, would it come to an end one day, and so on. So the Buddha told a story of a man who was shot with a poisoned arrow. A doctor arrived and offered to pull the arrow out. The man said, "Wait! Not until you tell me: Who shot the arrow? What type of bow did he use? What was the arrow made of? What kind of poison was used?" While asking these questions, he died. The Buddha said that likewise, questions about the nature of the universe and other speculative questions were not helpful in achieving release from our suffering.

ZEN UNLEASHED

Enjoying a nap
Mail carrier on the porch!
I bark my brains out

Non-Attachment Versus Detachment

Since the Buddha said that suffering is caused by desire, you might come to the conclusion that Buddhism promotes detachment—a cold, dispassionate separation from the rest of the world, having no desires.

Quite the contrary.

Buddhism promotes *non*-attachment, which is very different from detachment. Non-attachment is total engagement and flexibility in the world without being hindered or encumbered by our wants and desires. So when the mailman steps onto our front porch, I practice non-attachment to my cozy nap, jump up, and give warning!

ZEN UNLEASHED

Already shiny
Nothing to remove or clean
Why all this shampoo?!

. . . .

The Three Poisons

The Buddha taught that we are all inherently perfect, right now, but that we keeping forgetting this fact because of the three poisons: greed, aversion, and ignorance. These three poisons affect our behavior and cause us to veer off the eightfold path. Although there is one historical Buddha, in effect everyone is a Buddha struggling with the three poisons.

The Buddha defined ignorance as the deep-rooted belief that we are separate from everything and everyone else. From ignorance arise the other two poisons: greed, which the Buddha defined as craving what we don't have, and aversion, which he defined as craving to avoid what we dislike. When we are no longer swayed off the eightfold path by the three poisons, we are truly Buddhas.

At that point, in my opinion, baths become unnecessary.

ZEN UNLEASHED

. . . .

Like spirited leaves
Falling—the birds flutter down
And drink from my bowl

. . . .

Nirvana

I am normally possessive of my water bowl. One moment I'm sitting here, and the birds are over there. Then suddenly they fly to my water bowl and start bathing in it.

Grrrrrr!

Sometimes, though, a flash of clarity brings great peace. I realize there's no separation between the birds, the water bowl, and me. I experience the now without thinking of myself or others. There's just this moment.

When the Buddha talked of nirvana, he wasn't referring to a magical place that we go. Instead, he described nirvana as the extinguishing of the deep-rooted belief that we exist independent and separate from everything else. Nirvana is the end result of the hard work and effort of following the eightfold path.

ZEN UNLEASHED

·················

For all breeds of dogs
♫ My dog's bigger than your dog ♫
Ken-L Ration Meal!

·················

Interdependence

For those of you not old enough to remember, that's a famous dog food jingle from the 1960s. Yes, in a haiku, of all places.

Some people are angered by big oil, conservatives, and pro-life groups. Others are angered by Greenpeace, liberals, and pro-choice groups. I'm angered by Ken-L Ration. During the 1950s, Ken-L Ration used horse meat in their dog food. This makes me growl!

However, the Buddha taught that everything is interdependent. Before Ken-L Ration went out of business, the company employed thousands of people. Because of these jobs, some workers were able to send their kids to college to become veterinarians. Some of these workers' kids instead went to work for different dog food companies, helping keep dogs healthy and hunger-free. Others even took jobs at the Food and Drug Administration. Now those people are working diligently to make sure the current major dog food companies aren't using horse meat anymore.

For me to growl at Ken-L Ration, I would also have to growl at veterinarians, the FDA, and my current tasty dog food. A good argument to stop growling at things, I think.

ZEN UNLEASHED

. . . .

This fish I roll in
Decaying and rotting for
Ten thousand eons

. . . .

Karma

The Buddha taught that our thoughts and speech influence our actions and that for every action there is a consequence. Repeated actions form habits—sometimes good ones, sometimes bad. The Buddha also said the consequences of our actions have the potential to last a very long time. This connection between our thoughts, speech, actions, and their results is what the Buddha called karma.

Here's an example of how karma might work: You start thinking about biting the mail carrier. This leads you to bark a lot about it. Next, all your barking gets you so worked up that you actually bite a mail carrier.

What now?

The consequences follow. The mail carrier refuses delivery to your home, and Master is not pleased. When Master takes you to obedience school, you form a new habit and learn to refrain from biting. Positive consequences happen when the postal service begins delivering Master's mail again.

Ironically, the mail includes an expensive bill from the obedience school.

ZEN UNLEASHED

. . . .

Under the table
I receive squash, peas, meatloaf
Praise be the grandkids!

. . . .

Vegetarianism

You might be aware that the Buddha was a vegetarian. However, you might not know that he wasn't too uptight about it. Out of compassion for living things, he normally would not eat meat. However, when he was a guest at someone's home, he would eat with thanks whatever was offered.

Sounds good to me.

ZEN UNLEASHED

The stuffed Fido sits
Atop the grandkids' toy box
He doesn't eat much

. . . .

Buddha Statues

Master once brought home a stuffed-animal dog. I was a little miffed. Wasn't the real thing good enough? Then the grandkids played so roughly with the new stuffed dog that one of its eyes popped out. Whoa! My jealousy disappeared.

After Master repaired the eye, the grandkids began to treat the toy more respectfully. Thankfully, they also stopped yanking my tail. Perhaps they were afraid it would fall off? By learning to be respectful to a toy dog, they became more respectful of the real thing.

Buddha statues work in much the same way. The statues are not objects to be prayed to or to be worshiped. Instead, they offer an opportunity to show respect and appreciation for the Buddha and his teachings. Hopefully, such respect translates into respecting everyone in our life.

The jolly, chubby Buddha statue you may see from time to time, especially in Chinese restaurants, is Laughing Buddha—a Chinese legendary figure reputed to go around all year handing out gifts to children. If you rub his tummy, you will receive good luck. From what I have heard, you get even more luck when you rub a dog's tummy.

ZEN UNLEASHED

. . . .

Looking for my ball
Eyes glued to Master's finger
This will take a while

. . . .

Don't Cling to the Teaching

The Buddha told a story of a man who wanted to cross a turbulent river, yet there was no bridge in sight. So the man built a raft using reeds, sticks, and branches. After he successfully reached the other side, he noted how helpful the raft had been. So he decided to carry it around with him wherever he went. The Buddha noted that this wasn't very smart.

The Buddha was concerned that we might hold his teaching in such high regard that it would become a burden, like the raft became for the man in the story. Consequently, he made it clear that his teaching wasn't a Holy Truth to cling to, but instead was a means to help us become awakened.

Similarly, when Master is pointing at my ball, it is of no use to sniff his finger and stare at it. The finger is only a means to help me find the ball! It took me years to figure that out.

. . . .

I play with the toy,
Chase and pounce; if he wishes
Master can join me

. . . .

Inspire by Example

Among Buddhists, attempting to convert others to Buddhism is considered tacky at best, and abusive at worst. Buddhists believe, as in this haiku, that it's better to lead by example and let others come to you if they have an interest.

Master learned this when he tried to switch dog foods on me. I refused to try the new food because it smelled different. He got angry and yelled at me, which made me even less interested. But then Master got down on his hands and knees, stuck his face in my food, lifted his head, and said, "Mmm-mmm! Yummy!"

This gave me pause. Master had never eaten my dog food before, and seemed to find the food tasty. So I gave it a try.

Well, what do you know? It was pretty good.

PART TWO

. . . .

The Bare Bones of Zen

ZEN UNLEASHED

. . . .

Dirt and mud cake paws
I dig for my precious bone
It awaits inside

. . . .

Eihei Dogen and the Backward Step

A lthough there was just one historical Buddha, over the years different schools of Buddhism have emerged, each stressing different aspects of the eightfold path. In thirteenth-century Japan, a man by the name of Eihei Dogen founded the Soto Zen School.

Dogen encouraged the study of Buddhist texts, but he also recognized that the Buddha himself had achieved his awakening not through study, but through meditation. So the Soto Zen School put great emphasis on the parts of the eight-fold path dealing with meditation and mental development (right effort, right mindfulness, and right concentration).

In his essay *The Fukanzazengi*, Dogen encouraged his students: "You should therefore cease from practice based on intellectual understanding, pursuing words and following after speech, and learn the backward step that turns your light inwardly to illuminate your self. Body and mind of themselves will drop away, and your original face will be manifest."

Original face? What's that? It's a wonderful bone for all of us to try to find.

. . . .

Hysteric barking
Eyes wild with blind certainty
Nothing there but air

. . . .

Beginner's Mind

Our opinions are among our strongest attachments. With attachment to opinions, we become "experts."

Shunryu Suzuki (1904-1971), the Zen teacher from Japan who introduced Soto Zen to America, said, "In the beginner's mind there are many possibilities. In the expert's, there are few." Consequently, Suzuki encouraged his students to keep their beginner's mind at all times.

Let me be clear: it *is* okay to have opinions. However, our opinions, like us, change over time and have no solid existence. So instead of keeping a tight grip on our opinions, it is best to have some healthy skepticism about them.

And to avoid great embarrassment and humiliation, steer clear of fanatical certainty. Sometimes when you bark, there really isn't anyone there!

ZEN UNLEASHED

. . . .

Lost, cold, and hungry
The police dog and show dog
Find food together

. . . .

Zen's Relationship with Other Religions

The police dog and show dog may seem as different as dogs can be, but in the plight of suffering, they are the same. The experience of being lost, cold, and hungry is miserable for each. Furthermore, each can help the other without trying to "convert" the other to their manner of dog.

At Zen Centers, followers of other religions are always welcome. One hopes that the Buddha's teaching can help people in their own religious practices. For example, Christianity teaches, "Love your enemy." What a good teaching! It's pretty difficult to practice, though, because of a number of normal human attachments. If the Buddha's teachings about attachments can help a Christian become a better Christian, then some major tail wagging is in order.

. . . .

Back straight, head erect
Supporting the universe
The treat on my nose

. . . .

Zazen Meditation Postures

In *zazen* (Zen meditation) we sit in one of several upright positions. There are many postures, but the most common are the half-lotus and *seiza*. (See illustrations next two pages.) Note that one's tail end sits on a cushion to help maintain good posture and a straight back. The goal of these postures is to be comfortable and alert while not moving for long periods of time.

The full lotus posture is considered the most stable. However, unless you're very limber, it can be quite uncomfortable. For dogs it's pretty much impossible. Also, I do not recommend trying zazen while lying on the living room sofa with one's head on a pillow, belly to the sky, in the sun, even if it's quiet and no one else is home. One tends to fall asleep.

ZAZEN POSTURES

YES

Half-Lotus

YES

Full Lotus-People

NO

Full Lotus-Dogs

ZEN UNLEASHED

. . . .

Alongside Master
Window down, my head sticks out
One day I will drive

. . . .

The Student-Teacher Relationship

There is nothing like riding in the car with Master with my head sticking out the window. At that point it is clear that he is not just Master, but an admirable friend. I observe what he does and hope that one day I will be the one driving the car. I do worry about not having thumbs, though.

The Buddha's disciple Ananda once said, "This is half of the holy life: admirable friendship, admirable companionship, admirable camaraderie." The Buddha replied, "Don't say that. They're actually the whole of the holy life. When a monk has admirable people as friends, companions, and comrades, he can be expected to develop and pursue the noble eightfold path."

The student-teacher relationship in Zen is one in which the teacher is a spiritual friend. At Zen Centers, the teacher will do zazen with the students. Afterward, they might do some cleaning or fix-it jobs together, then sit down for tea.

The teacher may be knowledgeable in the Buddha's teachings and be a source of inspiration and a guide. But the teacher is not a guru, controlling leader, or strict obedience school instructor.

ZEN UNLEASHED

. . . .

Like a child chasing
Lost balloons floating away
I follow the birds

. . . .

Zazen and Our Attachments

When we sit zazen, we just observe our breath, awake to the moment. When thoughts arise, we simply return to observing the breath, without self-criticism, letting go of the thoughts in the process.

Sometimes zazen is quiet and peaceful. At other times, however, it's as if an entire flock of birds has landed in our backyard. It is difficult to sit still, and we are tempted to chase them around—just as we may be tempted to chase our thoughts during zazen. We may think, "I'll just follow these thoughts for a few moments longer, and then return to the breath." Then on we go with reminiscing, or planning, or judging, or recalling some injustice and its corresponding soap opera.

Instead, at the moment that we awaken to our wandering mind, we should endeavor to let go and return to the breath. Our strongest attachments often arise in our mind during zazen. Here is a great opportunity to practice letting go of them.

ZEN UNLEASHED

. . . .

One leg curls, tail stiff
The universe disappears
Only the pheasant

. . . .

Taking Zazen into Our Daily Life

Doing zazen on a meditation cushion means nothing if we don't take this practice into our daily life. This is a key point. When eating, napping, scratching, looking for a toy, barking at a mail carrier—really, anytime, anywhere—we endeavor to be awake in the present moment, focused on our surroundings, our thoughts, and our emotions.

It is not Zen practice to eliminate thinking. Thinking is a natural and necessary function of the mind. For example, if you need to figure out how to get your tie-out cable untangled from a bush, then go ahead and think it out. Just be awake and aware while you're doing it, not daydreaming about other things—like how you'd rather be taking a nap.

ZEN UNLEASHED

. . . .

The fleas bite my tail
My head continues to eat
This tasty supper.

. . . .

Experience the Meal

Why are the fleas biting my tail? How come fleas don't bite
the other dogs as much? How many fleas are on me? When
will they go away? Do some fleas like cats better? Do fleas
have families? How do they reproduce, anyway?

No, no, no, no, no! Wake up and completely experience
each moment in your life. Just eat!

ZEN UNLEASHED

Following a scent
Trying hard to be quiet
Crunch, crunch go the leaves

Be Awake to Our Emotions

Sometimes I like to sneak up on squirrels, just to see how close I can get before they run up a tree. During autumn, there is the added challenge of being quiet amongst the fallen leaves.

To be very, very quiet, I need to be completely awake in the moment.

Being awake in the moment is difficult when I am not awake to my emotions. Impatience, excitement, pride, anxiety—these are all emotions I may feel when sneaking up on a squirrel. If I'm not aware of them, my mind is distracted, and the leaves are crunching louder than squeak toys.

Take, for example, the story of the four monks who, as part of their awareness practice, took a vow to be silent for the day. They had been successful and were walking back to their cabin in the dark. Suddenly, a gust of wind blew one of the monk's lanterns out. "My light went out," he exclaimed. "Hey, be quiet!" said the second monk. The third monk scolded them, "You two idiots, now you've ruined it for the rest of us." Then the fourth monk declared, "Ha! I'm the only one who hasn't talked yet." The emotions of surprise, irritation, contempt, and pride had snuck up on the day of silence.

ZEN UNLEASHED

. . . .

Master comes home tired
I jump on him, tail wagging
He wags his tail back

. . . .

The Half-Smile Practice

The Zen teacher Thich Nhat Hanh (1926–) recommends a mindfulness practice of maintaining a half-smile. You can half-smile when you're first waking up in the morning, during free moments of the day, when you're irritated, or when you're doing zazen. The half-smile practice may seem trivial, but it melts the tension on your face and can change your entire attitude. Also, the half-smile can affect everyone around you in a positive manner.

For dogs, of course, it is different. A slight, steady tail wag throughout the day is recommended. Obviously, when Master comes home, it is acceptable for the tail to go full throttle.

ZEN UNLEASHED

. . . .

I chase the Frisbee
No purpose to this dumb game
Leap! Snap! Bring it home!

. . . .

Zazen is Not About Attaining Something

I used to wonder why I chased Frisbees. What was I trying to accomplish; what was my goal? Then I had a realization. I did it because it was a lot of fun. That's all!

If you are really into accomplishing things, then zazen—sitting, staring at a wall, and doing nothing—may be difficult at first. Doing zazen is not about trying to attain something. As the Zen teacher Sawaki Roshi (1880–1965) once said, "We don't eat food in order to poop, and we don't poop in order to make manure." Likewise, we don't sit zazen in order to become enlightened, or for any other reason. Zazen is a complete activity by itself.

ZEN UNLEASHED

. . . .

This leash that restrains
Like high banks of a river
Does liberate me

. . . .

The Ten Buddhist Precepts

A river is alive, vibrant, powerful. But without the restrictions of the banks, the river becomes like a tipped-over water bowl. In Zen practice we do our best to follow ten precepts. These precepts are not commandments from above, nor are we expected to succeed in following them 100 percent of the time. Rather, they are a measuring stick to gauge our practice.

1. Avoid killing.
2. Avoid stealing.
3. Avoid misuse of sex.
4. Avoid lying.
5. Avoid indulging in intoxicants.
6. Avoid speaking of the faults of others.
7. Avoid praising yourself while putting down others.
8. Avoid being stingy, including with Buddhist teaching.
9. Avoid indulging in anger.
10. Avoid slandering the Three Jewels (Buddha, Dharma, and Sangha).

So how are you doing on these ten today? How about compared to last month? Last year? When we pay attention, we can spot problems growing in our practice and begin to address them.

Recently, I have started to secretly hoard Master's socks. What's this all about? I need to meditate.

ZEN UNLEASHED

. . . .

Sit, stay, heel and beg
Master chatters endlessly
He's not enlightened.

. . . .

Focus on Your Own Practice

It is certainly easier to see the flaws in others than in yourself. That's the reason for this Zen teaching: You have enough things in your own practice to focus on, so don't be worrying about someone else's.

The Golden Rule—treat others as you wish to be treated—is a teaching that all major religions share. Unfortunately, in practice, it seems the Busybody Rule is just as popular. For example, I am always amused by the neighborhood dog who keeps barking at me because he thinks I'm barking too much. Really, now.

ZEN UNLEASHED

. . . .

Lassie saves the child
Dogs on TV don't have to
Come when they are called

. . . .

The Spirit of the Law

In the TV show *Lassie* (1954–1973), the collie Lassie would often ignore commands and do what she wanted, like save the boy Timmy from drowning in a lake. Then she would be praised. Since Master never praised me for disobeying a command, I thought for years that this was just a double standard allowed for rich and famous dogs. Then I came upon the following Zen story.

Once there were two monks walking down a road. They came across a young, beautiful woman who was having difficulty getting past a muddy spot in the road. The younger of the two monks lifted her up and across, then bid her on her way. The older of the two monks was livid. The Buddha had given instructions that monks should never touch a woman. A few miles down the road, he could no longer contain himself and scolded the younger monk: "What in the world were you doing, touching that young woman?!" The younger monk replied, "I put her down on the other side of the mud. Why are you still carrying her?"

Now I understood. By not touching the woman to help her across the mud, the older monk had followed the letter of the law. The younger monk, on the other hand, had wisely followed the spirit of the law...just like Lassie!

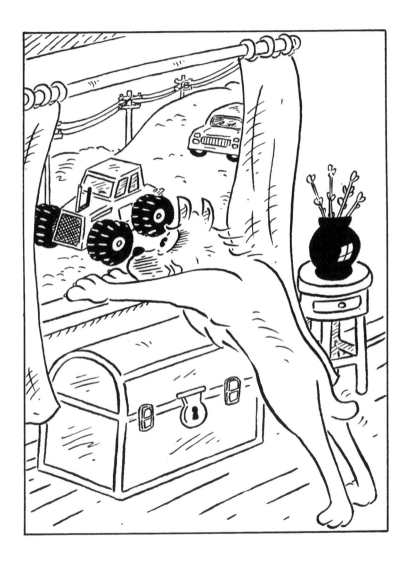

ZEN UNLEASHED

. . . .

I watch the traffic
Rumble past my house – large farm
Equipment must die!!

. . . .

Dealing with Anger

The Zen teacher Ichu, who lived in China during the four-teenth and fifteenth centuries, was once prompted by a student to write something of great wisdom. With his brush he wrote one word: "Attention." The student prompted for more. He then wrote: "Attention. Attention." The student, a little irritated, said, "That doesn't seem profound or subtle to me." So Ichu then wrote, "Attention. Attention. Attention." The frustrated student demanded to know what this "attention" was supposed to mean. Ichu replied, "Attention means attention."

In order to be awake—to be a Buddha right here and now—we need to learn to pay attention and develop our awareness. One place our awareness (or lack thereof) really shows is when we're dealing with anger.

When anger arises, we often act impulsively, without awareness, and hence without wisdom. One thing that really riles me up is large farm equipment driving past my home. Imagine if I followed my immediate impulse and gave chase. Who do you think would win?

Things go much better if I am paying attention and can catch my anger just as it begins to rise. Then, before my emotions get out of hand, I can make a decision based on choice rather than impulse—like deciding not to attack the combine harvester.

ZEN UNLEASHED

. . . .

In the nighttime breeze
Dogs howl in the night
I bark back incessantly

. . . .

Zen Rituals

A haiku is comprised of three lines. The first line contains five syllables, the second line has seven, and the last contains five again: five-seven-five. But what if all haiku were five-five-seven, like this one? I think it sounds just fine, but I'm sure if all the haiku in this book were like this, you would feel as if you had been ripped off.

This reminds me of my two favorite dog toys. I normally sleep with my Captain Kurklops Green Alien Dog Toy and save my chewing for my Giggling Carrot. However, my world would not end if I snuggled my carrot toy and chewed on Captain Kurklops.

The same concept applies to ritual in Zen practice. For example, it is common to ring a bell three times at the start of zazen and to ring it once at the end. But the ringing ritual could happen the other way around. There is nothing magic going on.

ZEN UNLEASHED

···············

Filled with oxygen
Lacking nothing—except food—
My bowl is empty

···············

The Heart Sutra and the Stomach Sutra

A sutra is a Buddhist teaching that is often chanted during religious services. The Heart Sutra is the most well known sutra used by the Zen school. This sutra focuses on the concept of emptiness—that all things are empty of independent, permanent existence. Here's an excerpt:

Form does not differ from emptiness.
Emptiness does not differ from form.
The same is true of feelings, perceptions, impulses,
   consciousness.
All things are marked by emptiness;
They neither appear nor disappear,
Are not tainted nor pure,
Do not increase nor decrease.

Zen students may spend their entire lifetime trying to fully understand the teaching of the Heart Sutra. I decided to rewrite the sutra in a topic more familiar to me. I call it the Stomach Sutra. Here's an excerpt:

A full bowl does not differ from an empty bowl.
An empty bowl does not differ from a full bowl.
The same is true for dog treat containers, plates, garbage
  cans, and kitchen floors.
All places where food can be found are marked by
  emptiness.
They do not appear nor disappear,
Are not filled with tainted food nor pure food,
Do not increase their storage of food nor decrease their
  storage.

When I am really hungry, I silently chant this sutra, and it buys me a couple of minutes.

ZEN UNLEASHED

. . . .

Unexpected bliss
On the path of wildflowers
Such fragrant urine

. . . .

Beware of Labels

People often like to label things. "This is beautiful. This is ugly." The label is not reality. Unfortunately, it is often interpreted that way.

The label also implies a permanence that does not exist. As the Buddha taught, everything is constantly changing. When we don't understand this, we attach to the label and cause suffering. Here's a classic example: "He's a bad dog." How many of my fellow dogs have borne the weight of this one? When such a label is applied, a dog's reputation may be ruined, even if he is a good dog at heart or works hard to become one.

The label "smells like urine" may seem clearly negative to you. But in my own personal experience, that is simply not the case. We should be very careful not to become too attached to the labels that we hear or use.

ZEN UNLEASHED

. . . .

Paws twitch in my sleep
While I dream that the vacuum
Has sucked up the cat!

. . . .

The Labels of "Good" and "Bad"

People often wonder what dogs dream about. When our paws start to twitch in our sleep, people seem especially curious about whether we're having a good dream or a nightmare.

Well, once I had a dream that a stray cat had snuck into our house, and the vacuum cleaner had taken care of business. A good dream, then? Maybe. My dream continued, and Master found the cat in the vacuum, felt sorry for the cat, and then invited it to live in our house. Ah, so a nightmare, you say? Maybe. In the dream I began to actually like the cat, and we became best friends. So, a good dream? Maybe. Later in the dream, the cat was on the road being chased by large farm equipment, and because I had grown fond of the cat, I went out to rescue him. The farm equipment's huge tires sprayed me with road gravel, resulting in dozens of cuts and bruises. Clearly a nightmare, right? Ah, but still later in the dream some dognappers from the circus came in the dead of night to steal me away. However, they didn't take me because I was wearing one of those ridiculous circular head guards that prevents you from licking your wounds and makes you walk into everything. So in the end a good dream, right? Well, I woke up then, but, good grief, who can say what was next?!

All in all, this is a fine example of why we shouldn't take too seriously the labels of "good" and "bad."

ZEN UNLEASHED

. . . .

The syllables of this haiku
Are all messed up
I'm only a dog

. . . .

Eighty Percent is Perfection

There is a saying in Zen: "Eighty percent is perfection." This speaks to our expectations, and encourages us to give ourselves a break. Instead, if we direct our efforts toward attaining perfection—the 100 percent kind—then we are heading down the wrong path.

Indeed, the Buddha's second noble truth was not "Suffering is caused by our imperfections." No, he taught that suffering is caused by desire. This includes desiring to attain perfection.

Also, our idea of what constitutes perfection is just that: our idea. Is perfection catching every Frisbee? Is it catching every Frisbee with style? Catching Frisbees faster than other dogs? What criteria shall we use to judge ourselves?

I should note that the saying is not "Fifty percent is perfection." There are limits, you know.

ZEN UNLEASHED

. . . .

Just a little rug
Nothing else to complicate
My simple doghouse

. . . .

Zen and Simplicity

Zen teaching and its emphasis on simplicity heavily influenced the Japanese art of flower arranging and the Japanese tea ceremony. Zen has also influenced the art of decorating, with the idea that one favorite item in a room gathers complete attention, whereas one hundred favorite items tend to be just a big mess.

So it is with my doghouse, which is quite Zen, as they say. I do wish it had some air conditioning, though.

ZEN UNLEASHED

Lush, green, and healthy
The grass at my outdoor run
I compost a lot

. . . .

Zen and the Environment

Please don't expect me to explain what I mean by "compost." This is one of those times to just read between the lines.

You don't need to read between the lines, however, to know that Buddhism promotes environmental responsibility. Everything is interconnected and interdependent, so taking care of the environment is no different from taking care of ourselves. As the Dalai Lama (1935–) said, "If we exploit the environment in extreme ways, we will suffer, as will our future generations. When the environment changes, the climatic condition also changes. When the climate changes drastically, the economy and many other things change. Our physical health will be greatly affected. Again, conservation is not merely a question of morality, but a question of our own survival."

ZEN UNLEASHED

．．．．．．．．．．．．．．．．．

The skunk's awful spray
I find myself wishing that
My self was not here

．．．．．．．．．．．．．．．．．．

Koans

Some Zen teachers give their students a koan to focus on during zazen. A koan is a problem that challenges the student to deeply experience no-self. Here are two famous koans:

What is the sound of one hand clapping?
What was your face before your parents were born?

Whoa! How could there be answers to these questions? Well, solving a koan is a lot like learning how to laugh. If you had never laughed before, you would not be able to discover how to laugh using logic. Real laughter would instead come spontaneously and provide direct insight of what laughter is. Direct insight, not logic, is what's needed to solve a koan.

A Zen student will work on his or her koan for months or even years until the teacher approves their answer. I myself have yet to solve a koan. For that matter, I also haven't figured out how to laugh, but Master says that has to do with a lack of proper vocal cords. I agree. On the inside, I'm laughing all the time!

ZEN UNLEASHED

. . . .

Can't leave and can't stay
Trapped by the dogcatcher's net
How do I get out?

. . . .

Life Koans

Koans may seem very confusing. However, we find koans
that are easier to grasp—but still hard to solve—right in our
everyday lives. For example, imagine you're lost. (Not good.)
Now imagine that a dogcatcher traps you. (Also not good.) If
you had a chance to escape, would you take it? Or, consider a
more human example: You may not want to move to a nurs-
ing home, but you also don't want to be a burden on your
family. How do you respond?

I call these dilemmas "life koans." How do we approach
them? With the spirit of zazen practice—by letting go!

Sometimes our desires and opinions are engaged in an
unwinnable tug-of-war. When we drop the tug rope (chew
toy, sock, old towel) of desire and opinion, we experience the
dilemma without our self at the center. From this open, free
place, we can make a choice that's not muzzled by ego.

·················

Master is crying
As if a tail was stepped on
I must lick his face

·················

Compassion and the Bodhisattva Ideal

At the heart of Zen practice is the development of compassion. Compassion is essential for becoming what in Buddhism is called a Bodhisattva: someone who consistently places the happiness of others before his or her own.

Compassion begins with empathy. Ironically, empathy for others starts with our own pain. Someone steps on our tail, our dog food runs out, maybe a cat makes us look stupid one day. Because of these things, we can relate to the pain of others. Then when we see others who are suffering, we have a choice. In order to avoid feeling their pain, we can tuck our tail between our legs and run away. Or, we can choose to empathize, engage, and do what we can to help. Compassion isn't empathy alone; compassion is action.

ZEN UNLEASHED

. . . .

Squeak squeak goes the toy
I really must have that toy
Without it I die

. . . .

Wisdom

Along with compassion, wisdom is essential to become a Bodhisattva. Wisdom requires a gut-level understanding of suffering, which enables one to know how best to help others.

Suppose you knew a dog who was passionately begging for a certain squeak toy. Would you give it to him? Seems like a good idea, but what if he had immediately destroyed his last ten squeak toys? Compassion without wisdom might say, "Yes, give him the toy. It will make him happy!" The Buddhist teacher Chogyam Trungpa (1940–1987) called this "idiot compassion."

On the other hand, compassion *with* wisdom might say, "Hold on. The squeak toy isn't helping, and this whole pattern is pretty wasteful of nice squeak toys. Perhaps what this dog really needs is some attention!"

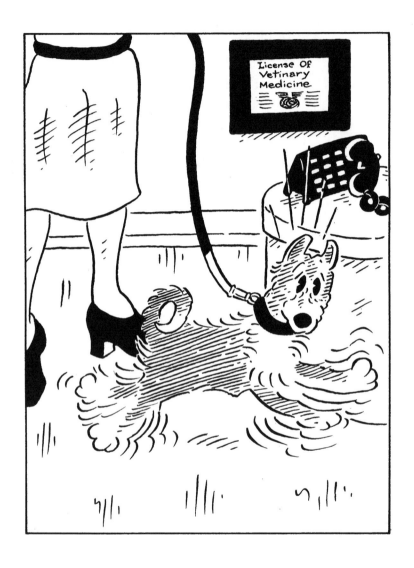

ZEN UNLEASHED

. . . .

Learning without words
Legs splay in four directions
Slick floor at the vet's

. . . .

The Importance of Personal Experience

When I was a pup, some neighbor dogs warned me that the floor at the vet's office was slippery. "Okay," I said, yawning. No, they barked, I didn't understand—it was *really* slippery. "Yeah, I get it," I replied. Be careful, they warned. "Yes, it's slippery, I'll be fine," I barked back. Then I got to the vet's office. Whoa! Holy cow! That floor is sliperrrrrrry!

There's nothing quite like actually experiencing something. You can read the Buddha's teaching and think it makes sense. But it's not until you actually start to practice Buddhism that it can really start to sink in. With that in mind, I encourage everyone to begin and maintain a meditation practice.

. . . .

Circling before sleep
Mindful of my surroundings
Like the wolves of old

. . . .

Lay Ordination

You may have wondered, "Why in the world do dogs circle several times before lying down?" It's a mindfulness exercise, spurred by millennia of scanning for cougars and other such dangers. So now you know.

In Zen, any effort toward maintaining mindfulness, non-attachment, compassion, and a meditation practice is something wonderful to bark about. As an optional part of the practice, some like to publicly declare this effort with the Zen lay ordination ceremony.

Just as when dogs circle before they sleep, this ceremony has an important connection to the past. At the end of the ceremony, the teacher presents the student with his lineage papers. The student's name is recorded at the bottom of the document. Above the student's name is recorded the name of the teacher. Above the teacher's name is the teacher's teacher, and so on. The very first name on the list is Siddhartha Gautama: the Buddha.

ZEN UNLEASHED

. . . .

They growl, so I growl
Storm clouds reflect on the lake –
Gentle swans bring peace

. . . .

Buddhism, Social Activism, and World Peace

Dear reader, I would like to share with you an issue close to my heart and encourage you to take action.

Dogfighting is reality for tens of thousands of dogs. These dogs are often kept isolated in chains with poor care. Their only interaction with people is in training for violence, and their only interaction with other dogs is in fights.

If they win, they will only be forced to fight again. Losers often do not survive their injuries. If they do survive, the punishment that comes from their handlers often finishes them off. It is difficult to imagine a more horrible fate for dogs: a fate in which their inborn love, joy, and carefree nature is beaten and brainwashed out of them.

The Humane Society of the United States (humanesociety.org) does a wonderful job battling against the tragedy of dogfighting. They offer a standing $5,000 reward for information that leads to the conviction of a dogfighter. Also, the nonprofit Knock Out Dog Fighting program (knockoutdogfighting.org) has done a wonderful job working with teens and addressing the root causes of dogfighting while not passing judgment on those involved. I encourage you to support these two groups and others like them.

But here's an important point. When the Buddha talked about creating peace in this world, he emphasized that peace must begin with us. For example, imagine you're at a rally protesting dogfighting, and some dogfighting supporters show up to counter-protest. Now imagine screaming and yelling and making threats against them.

Whoa! That's not bringing peace into the world, and it's not the Buddha's way. So my final words are to encourage you to take action against injustices you see in the world, but to do so in a peaceful, nonviolent way.

Oh, yes—and one last, very important thing. Seriously, pay attention here. This comes personally from the Buddha himself.

Dogs really, really, really love being scratched behind the ears.

About the Authors

Sheila currently resides at her home in Iowa. Like most dogs, she lives by Buddhist principles, being in the now. When she's not napping, Sheila enjoys taking car rides, playing Frisbee, and barking at people and things.

As part of her Buddhist practice, Sheila is no longer chasing large farm equipment, and appears to be making an effort to be friendlier with the cat next door. This is hit and miss, though.

Tim Macejak began practicing Zen in the early 1980s and has alternated between formal practice at Zen Centers and an informal at-home practice. He currently is co-leader of a Buddhist

meditation group at the Anamosa Men's Reformatory and a member of the Cedar Rapids Zen Center. He is an employee of the United States Postal Service and a dog lover. He lives in Anamosa, Iowa, with his wife, Teresa.